Exploring the Dinosaurs of North America: 10 Iconic Species

North America boasts a rich history of dinosaurs, with a diverse array of species that once roamed its ancient landscapes. From fearsome predators to gentle herbivores, these creatures left an indelible mark on the continent's geological and paleontological record. In this book, we will explore 10 iconic dinosaurs that inhabited North America, shedding light on their characteristics, habitats, and significance in the study of prehistoric life.

1. <u>Tyrannosaurus rex</u>

Tyrannosaurus rex, often dubbed the "king of the dinosaurs," is perhaps the most famous dinosaur to have ever lived.

This formidable predator prowled the western regions of North America during the Late Cretaceous period, approximately 68 to 66 million years ago.

With its massive size, powerful jaws, and serrated teeth, T. rex was a formidable hunter capable of bringing down even the largest of prey.

Fossil discoveries suggest that Tyrannosaurus rex inhabited a variety of environments, including lush forests, river valleys, and coastal plains.

Its range extended from present-day Canada down to parts of Mexico, making it one of the most widespread carnivorous dinosaurs of its time.
 The discovery of well-preserved T. rex skeletons, such as "Sue" in South Dakota, has provided paleontologists with invaluable insights into the anatomy and behavior of these iconic predators.

2. <u>Triceratops</u>

Triceratops is another iconic dinosaur that lived in North America during the Late Cretaceous period.

Known for its distinctive frill and three facial horns, Triceratops was a herbivorous dinosaur that roamed the plains and woodlands of western North America.
Fossil evidence suggests that these dinosaurs congregated in herds and likely grazed on vegetation such as ferns, cycads, and conifers.

Triceratops was a contemporary of Tyrannosaurus rex, and fossilized remains of both species have been found in close proximity, leading to speculation about possible interactions between predator and prey.

Despite its formidable appearance, Triceratops may have used its horns primarily for defense against predators rather than for intra-species combat.

Fossilized footprints discovered in Colorado provide evidence of Triceratops' social behavior and gregarious nature.

3. <u>Stegosaurus</u>

Stegosaurus, with its distinctive double row of bony plates along its back and spikes on its tail, is one of the most recognizable dinosaurs of the Late Jurassic period.

Although primarily known from fossils found in western North America, including Colorado, Utah, and Wyoming, Stegosaurus likely inhabited a broader range across the continent. These herbivorous dinosaurs were well-adapted to a variety of environments, from forested regions to open plains.

One of the most intriguing features of Stegosaurus is its spiked tail, or "thagomizer," which may have served as a defensive weapon against predators such as Allosaurus.

Fossilized trackways discovered in Utah suggest that Stegosaurus moved in small herds, possibly foraging for food and seeking protection in numbers.
Despite its large size and imposing appearance, Stegosaurus was likely a relatively peaceful herbivore, content to browse on low-lying vegetation.

4. <u>Allosaurus</u>

Allosaurus was one of the top predators of the Late Jurassic period, dominating the landscapes of western North America approximately 155 to 150 million years ago.

With its razor-sharp teeth, powerful jaws, and agile build, Allosaurus was well-equipped to hunt a wide range of prey, including herbivorous dinosaurs such as Stegosaurus and Apatosaurus.

Fossil discoveries suggest that Allosaurus was a highly successful predator, with numerous specimens found in various states of preservation.

In addition to its formidable hunting abilities, Allosaurus may have also been a scavenger, opportunistically feeding on carrion when the opportunity arose. Despite its ferocious reputation, Allosaurus likely faced competition from other predators such as Ceratosaurus and Torvosaurus, as evidenced by fossilized remains found in close association.

5. **Velociraptor**

Velociraptor is perhaps best known for its portrayal in popular culture, thanks to its appearances in films such as "Jurassic Park."

However, the real Velociraptor was much smaller than its on-screen counterpart, reaching lengths of around 6 feet and weighing approximately 30 pounds. These agile predators lived in North America during the Late Cretaceous period, where they likely hunted in packs and targeted smaller prey such as small dinosaurs and early mammals.

Despite its diminutive size, Velociraptor was a formidable hunter, armed with sharp claws and keen senses.

Fossilized evidence suggests that Velociraptor may have been covered in feathers, further highlighting its close relationship to modern birds.

Although Velociraptor coexisted with larger predators such as Tyrannosaurus rex, it likely occupied a different ecological niche, focusing on smaller, more agile prey.

6. <u>Ankylosaurus</u>

Ankylosaurus was a heavily armored dinosaur that lived in North America during the Late Cretaceous period. Characterized by its thick, bony plates and club-like tail, Ankylosaurus was a formidable defensive herbivore that likely used its armored body to deter predators such as Tyrannosaurus rex.

Fossilized remains of Ankylosaurus have been found in various locations across western North America, including Montana, Wyoming, and Alberta, Canada.

These dinosaurs likely inhabited forested regions and lowland areas, where they could find ample vegetation to sustain their large bodies.

Despite their imposing appearance, Ankylosaurus may have been relatively slow-moving animals, relying on their armored plating and defensive weaponry to protect themselves from predators.

7. <u>Edmontosaurus</u>

Edmontosaurus was a large herbivorous dinosaur that lived in North America during the Late Cretaceous period.

With its duck-billed snout and toothless beak, Edmontosaurus was well-adapted to feeding on tough vegetation such as ferns, cycads, and conifers.

Fossilized remains of Edmontosaurus have been found in various locations across western North America, including Montana, Wyoming, and South Dakota.

These dinosaurs likely inhabited floodplain environments and river valleys, where they could find abundant plant material to sustain their massive bodies.

Despite their large size, Edmontosaurus may have been relatively agile animals, capable of moving on both two and four legs depending on the situation.

8. <u>Pachycephalosaurus</u>

Pachycephalosaurus was a dome-headed dinosaur that lived in North America during the Late Cretaceous period.

Characterized by its thick, bony skull and relatively small body, Pachycephalosaurus was likely an herbivorous dinosaur that fed on low-lying vegetation.

Fossilized remains of Pachycephalosaurus have been found in various locations across western North America, including Montana, Wyoming, and South Dakota.

These dinosaurs likely inhabited
forested regions and open plains,
where they could find ample
food and shelter.

Despite their relatively small
size, Pachycephalosaurus may
have been territorial animals,
using their thick skulls to engage
in intra-species combat and
establish dominance within their
social groups.

9. <u>Deinonychus</u>

Deinonychus was a small, agile predator that lived in North America during the Early Cretaceous period.

With its sharp claws and keen senses, Deinonychus was likely a formidable hunter capable of taking down prey much larger than itself.

Fossilized remains of Deinonychus have been found in various locations across western North America, including Montana, Wyoming, and Utah.

These dinosaurs likely inhabited forested regions and river valleys, where they could find ample cover and opportunities for ambush hunting.

Despite their relatively small size, Deinonychus may have hunted in packs, using teamwork and coordination to bring down larger prey.

10. <u>Diplodocus</u>

Diplodocus was a long-necked sauropod dinosaur that lived in North America during the Late Jurassic period.

With its elongated neck and tail, Diplodocus was one of the largest animals to have ever walked the earth, reaching lengths of up to 90 feet.

Fossilized remains of Diplodocus have been found in various locations across western North America, including Colorado, Utah, and Wyoming.

These dinosaurs likely inhabited open plains and forested regions, where they could find ample vegetation to sustain their massive bodies.

Despite their immense size, Diplodocus may have been relatively peaceful animals, using their long necks to reach high branches and feed on leaves and foliage.

In conclusion, the dinosaurs of North America represent a diverse array of species that once inhabited the continent's ancient landscapes.

From fearsome predators like Tyrannosaurus rex to gentle giants like Diplodocus, these creatures left an indelible mark on the continent's geological and paleontological record. By studying their fossils and reconstructing their lives, paleontologists continue to unravel the mysteries of North America's prehistoric past.

Please use the next few
pages for your notes and
debates.